# RACHEL CARSON

## PRESERVING A SENSE OF WONDER

FULCRUM

GOLDEN, COLORADO

*O*nce there was a child whose love of nature
would one day lead her to write a book that
changed our world.

On a little farm not far from a bend of the

Allegheny River, Rachel saw spring fog that

seemed to turn each road into a river and the

land back into an ancient sea.

That place was called Springdale, Pennsylvania,

a town once as lovely as its name. There,

in a clapboard house with four small rooms,

a wide-eyed girl learned from her mother the

names and songs of birds, and to see the spirit

in all living things.

While she would not see the ocean until she was a grown woman, books began to carry Rachel away to distant shores, where the music of waves would move her heart.

Although Rachel always knew her path would be that of a writer, she chose to study living things—biology—in college.

When at last Rachel made her first visit to the ocean
to work for one enchanted summer, her feet felt the
pull of Cape Cod's salty waves, and her wondering
eyes took in the great sea.

Sometimes nature lends a heart strength, and when
Rachel looked for her first job in science, her writing
saved the day. She would write radio scripts on the
romance of the waters, a subject close to her heart.

Later, she wrote her first book, *Under the Sea-Wind*, about her great love, the wonderful sea. In its pages, Rachel followed the creatures of ocean and shore throughout the seasons.

This was only the beginning of Rachel's true stories of nature's wonders—soon she wrote *The Sea around Us*, then *The Edge of the Sea*. Now she could write all the time and live in a cottage on the coast of Maine, where the ocean's song was always nearby.

In the Pennsylvania town where Rachel had spent her childhood, few trees were now left, the rivers were foul, the air was choked with smoke, and the gentle rain was now poisoned with sprays to kill insects.

When Rachel heard stories of robins dropping dead from eating insects treated with the chemical sprays, she could no longer be silent. She began to write a book that warned of a world where the songs of birds would disappear and the rivers and oceans would die.

Rachel's new book, *Silent Spring*, helped people understand that if we break one strand in the web of life, every other strand is in danger. While many powerful voices were raised against her, others read Rachel's words and felt their own hearts change.

Two years later, Rachel had cancer and felt her own life ending. Yet she felt peace and happiness because she knew that her books would be read by those who had never known her and that the living sea would still wash onto the shore.

Because of Rachel and her powerful words for
nature, the rivers of our land now flow cleaner,
the songbirds still sing from the apple trees, and
the fish still swim in Rachel's beloved sea.
And like Rachel, somewhere a child watches
and listens and cares for this earth as she keeps
her sense of wonder.

## MILESTONES

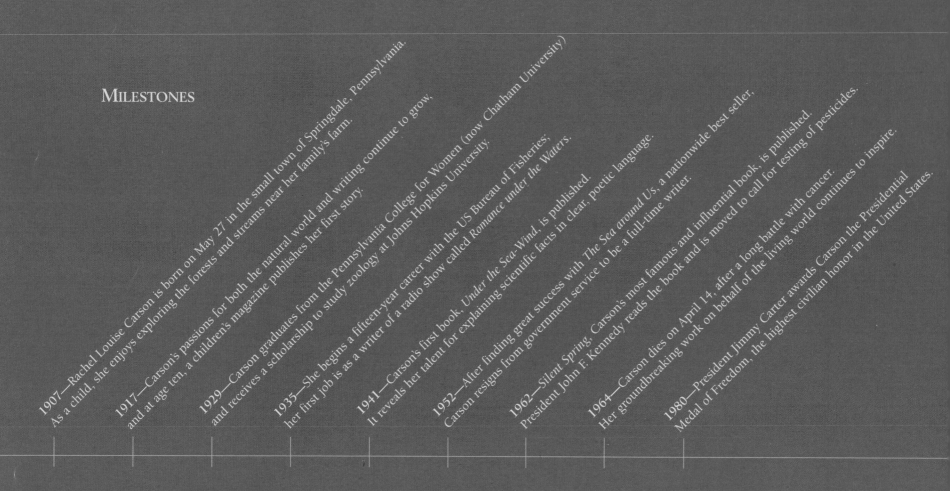

**1907**—Rachel Louise Carson is born on May 27 in the small town of Springdale, Pennsylvania. As a child, she enjoys exploring the forests and streams near her family's farm.

**1917**—Carson's passions for both the natural world and writing continue to grow, and at age ten, a children's magazine publishes her first story.

**1929**—Carson graduates from the Pennsylvania College for Women (now Chatham University) and receives a scholarship to study zoology at Johns Hopkins University.

**1935**—She begins a fifteen-year career with the US Bureau of Fisheries; her first job is as a writer of a radio show called *Romance under the Waters*.

**1941**—Carson's first book, *Under the Sea-Wind*, is published. It reveals her talent for explaining scientific facts in clear, poetic language.

**1952**—After finding great success with *The Sea around Us*, a nationwide best seller, Carson resigns from government service to be a full-time writer.

**1962**—*Silent Spring*, Carson's most famous and influential book, is published. President John F. Kennedy reads the book and is moved to call for testing of pesticides.

**1964**—Carson dies on April 14, after a long battle with cancer. Her groundbreaking work on behalf of the living world continues to inspire.

**1980**—President Jimmy Carter awards Carson the Presidential Medal of Freedom, the highest civilian honor in the United States.

Rachel Louise Carson was born May 27, 1907, on a farm in Springdale, Pennsylvania. When she was ten, *St. Nicholas*, the best of all children's magazines, published her first story. She majored in biology at Pennsylvania College for Women (now Chatham University), earned a master's degree in marine zoology at John Hopkins University, and went to work for the US Bureau of Fisheries writing radio scripts. Her books include *Under the Sea-Wind*, *The Sea around Us*, and *The Edge of the Sea*. She wrote books to teach young people about nature, including *Help Your Child to Wonder* and *A Sense of Wonder*. Her book *Silent Spring* was translated into more than fifteen languages and has been declared the most influential book of the past fifty years. She died in April 1964, after a long fight with breast cancer.

RACHEL CARSON WROTE EXTENSIVELY ABOUT NATURE.
HERE ARE A FEW SELECTIONS OF HER WORDS.

*Take time to listen and talk about the voices of earth and what they mean—the majestic voice of thunder, the winds, the sound of surf or flowing streams.*

*Every mystery solved brings us to the threshold of a greater one.*

*The lasting pleasures of contact with the natural world are not reserved for scientists but are available to anyone who will place himself under the influence of earth, sea, and sky.*

*A child's world is fresh and new and beautiful, full of wonder and excitement. It is our misfortune that for most of us that clear-eyed vision, that true instinct for what is beautiful and awe-inspiring is dimmed and even lost when we reach adulthood.*

*Those who contemplate the beauty of the earth find reserves of strength that will endure as long as life lasts.*

*If a child is to keep his inborn sense of wonder, he needs the companionship of at least one adult who can share it, rediscovering with him the joy, excitement, and mystery of the world we live in.*

*In every outthrust headland, in every curving beach, in every grain of sand there is the story of the earth.*

*The edge of the sea is a strange and beautiful place.*

*The more clearly we can focus our attention on the wonders and realities of the world about us, the less taste we shall have for destruction.*

Library of Congress Cataloguing-in-Publication Data

Locker, Thomas, 1937-
Rachel Carson : preserving a sense of wonder / by Thomas Locker and
Joseph Bruchac.
p. cm.
Summary: A biography of Rachel Carson interspersed with her own
memorable quotes.
ISBN-13: 978-1-55591-482-0 (hardbound : alk. paper)
ISBN-13: 978-1-55591-695-4 (paperback : alk. paper)
1. Carson, Rachel, 1907–1964—Juvenile literature. 2.
Biologists—United States—Juvenile literature. 3.
Environmentalists—United States—Juvenile literature. [1. Carson,
Rachel, 1907–1964. 2. Biologists. 3. Scientists. 4. Women—Biography.]
I. Bruchac, Joseph, 1942- II. Title.
QH31.C33L63 2004
333.95'16092—dc22

2003019346

*Design by Nancy Duncan*
Printed in China
0 9 8 7 6 5 4 3 2 1

Fulcrum Publishing
4690 Table Mountain Dr., Ste. 100
Golden, CO 80403
800-992-2908 • 303-277-1623
www.fulcrumbooks.com